What Goes On at a Radio Station?

What Goes On at a Radio Station?

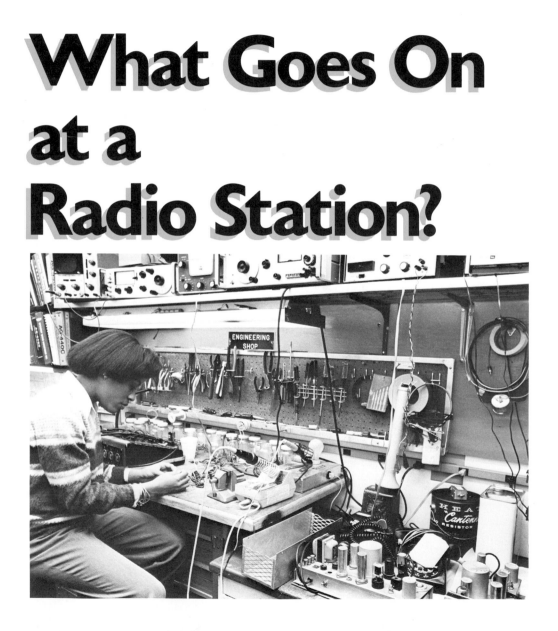

by Susan Gilmore

Carolrhoda Books, Inc.
Minneapolis

4239646

The author wishes to thank all the people at WCCO Radio, especially Jon Quick, Director of Advertising and Promotion, Phil Lewis, Vice President and General Manager, and Gordon A. Mikkelson, Director of Special Projects and Public Relations, for educating me, turning me into somewhat of a radio fanatic, and helping to make this book possible.

The glossary on page 40 gives definitions of words shown in **bold face** in the text.

Manufactured in the United States of America

Design by Gale Houdek

LIBRARY OF CONGRESS CATALOGING IN PUBLICATION DATA

Gilmore, Susan.
  What goes on at a radio station?

    Summary: Describes the activities at a large radio station and explains the jobs of broadcasters, engineers, meteorologists, and others involved in putting together a radio show.
    1. Radio broadcasting—Juvenile literature. 2. Radio—Vocational guidance—Juvenile literature. [1. Radio broadcasting. 2. Occupations] I. Title.

PN1991.57.G54   1984   384.54   83-18906
ISBN 0-87614-223-4 (lib. bdg.)

1 2 3 4 5 6 7 8 9 10 93 92 91 90 89 88 87 86 85 84

to my parents, John and Marcia Gilmore, my brother, John D.,
and my husband, John Paul Lauenstein

A Note from the Author

Every morning millions of people around the world wake up to the sound of music or conversation on their clock radios. They may listen to their radios as they cook breakfast, drive to work, walk down the street, do homework, or lie on the beach. Radio is everywhere. Day and night, stations are broadcasting music, news and weather reports, descriptions of sports events, interviews, and information about everything from community events to the price of hogs. People listen to their radios to relax, to learn, or simply for companionship.

The station I have chosen to interview and focus my camera on for this book is WCCO in Minneapolis, Minnesota. I chose it partly for its size. WCCO is a large station, affiliated with the CBS network, and therefore nearly everything that *can* happen at a radio station *does* happen there. I also chose it because it is one of the stations to which I have enjoyed listening. I have not tried to cover every single aspect of running a radio station, nor have I attempted to explain how radios work mechanically. Instead I have tried to give readers a picture behind the sounds and perhaps to excite someone's imagination about all the unseen people who make our daily lives so pleasant.

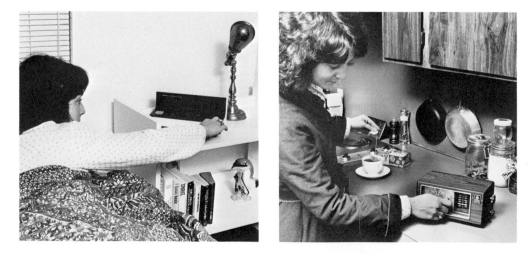

Contents

Announcers

The people on our radios with whom we are most familiar are called **announcers**. Announcers conduct interviews, introduce music to be played, inform us of local events, deliver many commercials, and sometimes give us news and weather reports as well. They make jokes and chat with us. They are the personalities we recognize.

Announcer Ruth Koscielak reads from the announcer's copybook...

...and crosses off the announcement in the DOS.

Every announcer begins each day by going over the Daily Operating Schedule, called the **DOS**, which lists everything that is to happen while the announcer is on the air: every announcement, program, commercial, and station break. When on the air, the announcer follows the DOS. When an announcement is scheduled, the announcer reads it from the **announcer's copybook**. This is a book filled with scripts for the various announcements and commercials. After each announcement in the DOS has been read, it is crossed off and signed by the announcer. Later the DOS will be checked and filed.

Charlie Boone (left) and Roger Erickson (center)
interview author Richard Reece.

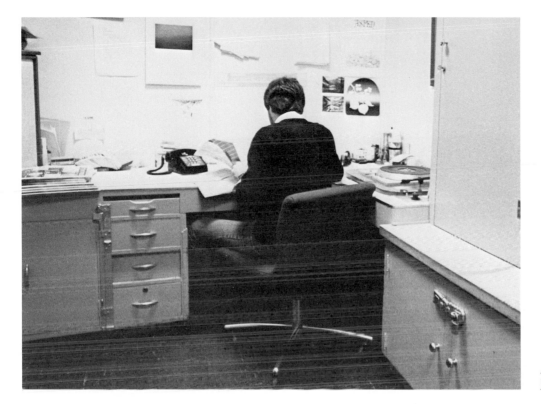

Announcer Denny Long spends many hours preparing for his show.

Many announcers interview people on the air, some of them in person, others over the telephone. For an in-person interview, the guest comes to the radio station. For a telephone interview, the guest is called from a telephone in the broadcasting studio.

Announcers may be on the air for only a few hours each day, or they may be on the air for many hours. In either case, they spend a lot of time off the air preparing for their shows. They rehearse stories and jokes they want to tell, they do research on their guests, they pick out music to be played, and they keep up with current news and local events. Even when a **newscaster** delivers regular news programs, the announcer has to keep listeners informed about news that has just happened and about weather, road, and travel conditions.

11

Producers

Although we don't often hear them, **producers** can have a great deal to do with many of the radio programs we enjoy. Producers are responsible for the programs assigned to them. They come up with ideas for the programs, discuss these ideas with the announcers involved, line up guests, and provide the announcers with as much information as possible about the people who will appear and the topics that will be discussed.

Producers work under the direction of the **program director**. The program director works with the directors of other departments, the station's **general manager**, and the station's owner to decide what sort of programming the station should be doing. They might decide that they want the station's major audience to be housewives or country music fans or people between the ages of 30 and 65. The station's programs will then be planned to appeal to that specific audience.

Producer Sue Frase is setting up a telephone interview that will begin
as soon as announcer Charlie Boone (center) and his guest are ready.

Sometimes a program takes place outside the radio station. For example, a program might feature interviews with people at a convention. Then the producer either arranges to broadcast from the convention hall or supervises the taping of that program to be broadcast later.

Producers have to be extremely well organized! Many other people at the station need to know what the producer has planned—the **traffic manager**, for example, who makes up the DOS. The producer keeps a large file of all upcoming program plans so that anyone can quickly find out what is scheduled.

It's important to mention that not all radio stations have producers. Small stations and stations that just play music usually do not. Instead, each announcer acts as his or her own producer.

Sue works with a technician on a taped interview.

Producers spend a lot of time on the telephone and writing letters.

This morning's guest is a children's choir. Sue scheduled this appearance months ago. This morning she met the children at the door and showed them into the studio. Now she is directing a choir member to the microphone.

Technicians

The technician, who sits in the **control room**, wears earphones in order to hear the announcer, who sits in another room. The technician in this photograph can see and hear two broadcasting rooms at once. A program announcer is in one room; a news announcer is in the other.

At most radio stations, the announcer, sometimes called a **disc jockey**, plays the records and runs the equipment, but at larger stations these jobs are done by the **technician**. Technicians, also called **engineers**, and announcers work together to control the sounds that you hear over the radio. If you hear the announcer sneezing while a record is being played, the announcer has made a mistake by forgetting to turn off his or her microphone. But if you hear a record being played at the wrong speed, the technician has made a mistake.

Technicians have other responsibilities as well. If an announcer is conducting a telephone interview, the technician is responsible for making sure that you can hear the person on the telephone clearly. Or perhaps the producer and announcer want background music during part of their program. The technician must run the music at the right time and make sure that you can still hear the announcer over it.

cassette players

cartridges of commercials, announcements, interviews, and news reports to be played

From the control room, technician Art Johnson can operate tape recorders, turntables, cassette cartridge players, telephone lines, and all of his other equipment.

Sometimes an announcer uses **prerecorded** (recorded ahead of time) announcements. Then the announcer doesn't have to read them on the air; the tape can be played instead. The technician both makes the recording and makes sure that it is played at the right time.

Technicians tape many other things as well. For example, a producer and announcer may want to interview someone who is not available when the show is on the air. The producer might then arrange for an interview at another time. A technician will tape that interview, then run it later when the show *is* on the air.

Like announcers, technicians follow a tight schedule. They operate a tape machine that records everything broadcast throughout each day. This enables the station to check back on what was on the air. Finally, technicians are responsible for keeping their equipment in good condition.

the technician's DOS and turntable

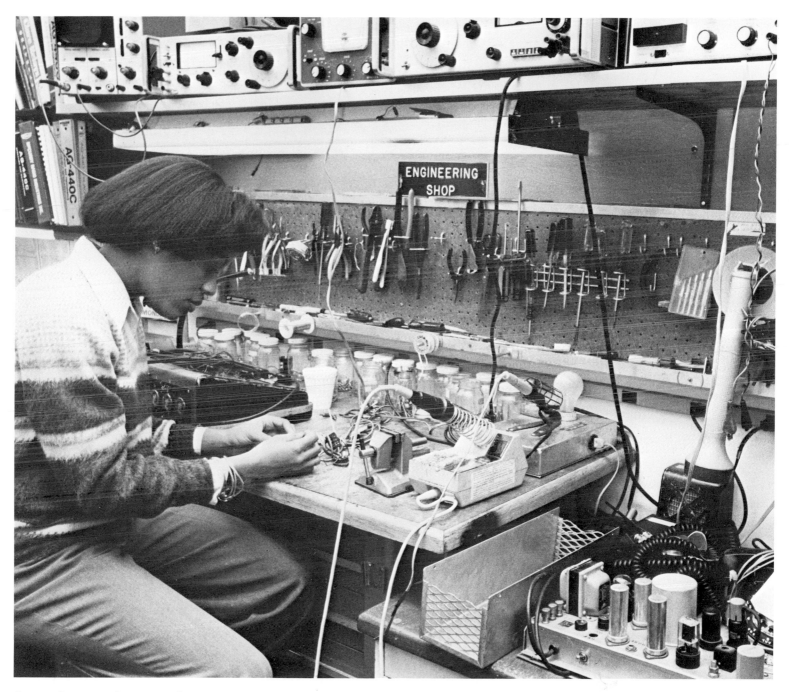

the technicians' repair shop

Preparing a tape to be broadcast later can sometimes look like a complicated process, but it's actually quite simple. This technician is working on a commercial that she recorded earlier. The station's sales department wants to eliminate some parts of it, so the technician must now get rid of those parts.

First she listens to the recording on a tape machine. When she finds the sections that are to come out, she marks them directly on the tape with a white marker. Then she cuts out the unwanted parts with a razor blade. She then tapes the tape back together again, leaving out the unwanted sections. This is called **splicing**. Material can also be added to the tape in this way.

Technician Yvonne Barrett reads her instructions.

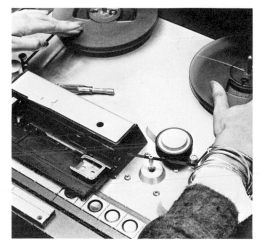  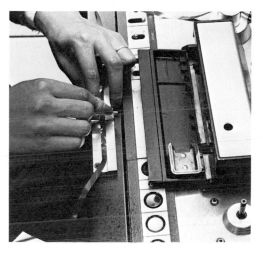

She finds the sections that are to come out of the tape,

marks a section to be eliminated,

and cuts that section out of the tape.

When she has spliced the tape back together again, she listens to it.

Remote Broadcasts

At a large radio station, many special events are **remote broadcasts**. The pictures here show a remote broadcast from a state fair. Days before the opening of the fair, a broadcasting studio was assembled and equipment installed and checked to make sure that it was in good working condition. Then during the fair the station broadcasts from the remote studio, giving people a chance to see and talk with their favorite radio personalities.

The announcers sit in the front of the studio where everyone can see them. The technician is at the control panel in the rear of the room. There is a second room in the studio for the station's newspeople, and a small storeroom as well.

Sports Broadcasts

Sports broadcasts of local, regional, and professional games are important to many radio listeners. Each sports broadcast takes many hours to prepare.

The sports producer is in charge, lining up special guests, arranging pre- and post-game programs, and sometimes arranging for a professional to comment on the game along with the announcer.

A technician has made certain that microphones have been placed in good positions. At a baseball game, for example, microphones might be set up in positions to pick up the roar of the crowd and the crack of the bat hitting the ball. When the game is on the air, a technician will be responsible for tuning in to the right microphone at the right time or blending the sounds from several microphones at once.

The announcer, usually called a **sportscaster**, has done a lot of preparation as well. Before the game starts, most sportscasters spend some time at the stadium interviewing the players, coaches, and spectators. These interviews are taped by the technician for broadcast later. In addition, the sportscaster must be sure to have up-to-date information on all the players in this game as well as a knowledge of what's going on in the rest of the league. The sportscaster often works with a **spotter** who identifies the players during the game and a **statistician** who provides the sportscaster with information about those players.

This radio station has permanent broadcasting booths in many sports arenas. In addition to the standard equipment, this booth is equipped with a **teletypewriter** on which current sports scores from all over the country are printed out on paper as they are reported. The broadcaster will check the printout throughout the game and give listeners the current scores on other games.

These two sportscasters are covering a football game.

This sportscaster is checking the teletypewriter.

The papers on this sportscaster's desk include the latest report off the teletypewriter, information sheets on the players in this game, and a written record of the plays that have been made so far.

The Music Library

One of the most awesome sights at a radio station is the music library. At a large station there will be thousands and thousands of records and tape cartridges stored on library shelves. Each one is cataloged in a manner similar to the way books are cataloged in a library. At a station that plays classical music, there may be 12 or 15 records of the same piece of music, each record featuring a different performer. Even at small radio stations the music library seems enormous.

The person in charge of organizing and maintaining the music library is called the music director. The music director also helps announcers choose which music will be played on the air. Every station works differently, but at this station the music director makes up a list of music every week for the announcers to choose from. The announcers make some of their selections from this list; the rest are up to them. Sometimes the music director also helps other station employees select suitable music or sound effects for commercials and announcements.

The music library must be kept up to date. Record companies send the station copies of their new releases and try to get the music director to persuade announcers to play their records. The director listens to dozens of new records each month and recommends which should be played on the station.

Music director Denny Long is also an announcer.

The Newsroom

One of the busiest places at a radio station is the newsroom. A radio news department must cover local, state, national, and international news. Where does all this news come from? When a station is affiliated with a large network (like CBS, NBC, or ABC), the network delivers reports from all over the world all day long. Both network stations and smaller stations use the services of Associated Press and/or United Press International, two large international news services. Reports from networks and news services come into the radio newsroom by way of teletypewriters and other equipment. These machines must be checked constantly so that important stories, like a presidential assassination attempt, can be rushed to the announcer on the air and read to listeners immediately. In addition, **reporters** are constantly searching for news stories, either over the telephone or out in the field.

The person who decides which stories will be reported on the air and which will not is called the **news editor**. News editors report to the **news director**.

A section of the newsroom, one of the busiest places at a radio station

Let's take a look at how a radio newsroom might cover an urgent story. The news editor has just learned that a man has taken several people hostage in a local hotel. The editor immediately telephones the local sheriff's office to confirm the story or assigns the job to one of the people working under him. The story is true, so the editor interviews several people at the sheriff's office over the phone. By pushing a button on his phone panel, the editor is able to record the interviews on a taping system connected to the telephone.

The hostage situation continues, so the editor decides to send a reporter to the scene to gather information and interview people. The reporter locates the hotel on a map, grabs a pad and pen for taking notes, checks to make certain that her tape recorder is working, and is on her way.

While the reporter is at the scene of the crime, the news editor listens to the tape of his telephone interviews. Not everything on the tape is worth broadcasting, so the editor **edits** the tape. After choosing which sections should be used and marking them on the tape, he delivers the tape to a technician. The technician will rerecord the tape onto a tape cartridge, including only the parts that the editor wants.

Time is short, so the reporter can't conduct all the interviews she would like and return to the newsroom in time to meet her deadline. She must call in quickly with the information she has been able to gather so far. She may even go on the air "live" with the story, either over the telephone or from a remote broadcast truck. The story is then typed up and delivered with the tape cartridge to the announcer on the air for repeat broadcasts. (A less important story would not be so rushed since it would be held for broadcast during a regularly scheduled news program.)

All this has taken only a matter of minutes, but the story isn't finished yet. The news department will continue to cover it until the hostage situation has been resolved.

The Weather Center

At this radio station the **meteorologist** (weather forecaster) broadcasts weather updates every hour. Four times each day he broadcasts longer reports. Any important news—a storm warning, for instance—is broadcast immediately, either by the meteorologist or by the announcer on the air at the time.

Meteorologists do not simply look out their windows and report whatever weather conditions they happen to see. They use a great deal of sophisticated equipment, and they work closely with the National Weather Service. The National Weather Service, operated by the federal government, keeps track of weather conditions, makes forecasts, and provides information to weather centers. The meteorologist uses the **national weather wire, weather radar screens, current surface maps machines,** and other equipment to gather weather information from all over the country.

The national weather wire sends reports and forecasts to the radio weather center over teletypewriters. In an emergency these typewritten reports can be ripped off the machine, raced to the announcer on the air, and read just as they are. Smaller stations may rely on the national weather wire almost completely for their weather reports.

Additional weather reports come into the weather center over weather radar screens. These are television screens that show the movement of any precipitation.

Current surface maps, which are diagrams of weather conditions, come into the weather center over the current surface maps machine. The maps can be ripped off the machine for further study.

It is the meteorologist's job to analyze all the weather information coming in and find the best way of presenting it to radio listeners.

Meteorologist Mike Lynch (right)
goes over weather maps...

...and checks the national weather
wire.

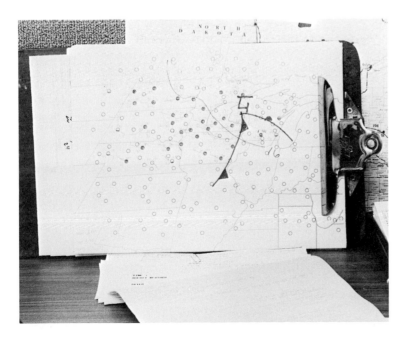

surface maps

The Sales Department

Running a radio station costs a great deal of money. Employees must be paid. Millions of dollars worth of equipment must be purchased and kept in tip-top shape. Where does a radio station get all the money it needs to operate? Public radio stations are supported by contributions from listeners and by grants from corporations. Commercial radio stations are supported through the sale of radio time to advertisers. Stations employ salespeople to sell that time.

Much of a salesperson's time is spent staying in contact with his or her clients (usually called **accounts**), either in person or on the telephone. Salespeople are always trying to develop new accounts as well.

When clients purchase radio time, they have specific needs they expect the radio station to meet. They may want their commercials delivered by a particular broadcaster or aired at a specific time of the day. Clients want to be involved in making their commercials as well. Some clients provide tapes of finished commercials. Others work with the radio station to create their commercials.

The sales department coordinates all these activities, supervises the production of commercials that will please their accounts, and makes sure that those commercials are aired at the right time.

Salesman Brad Johnson meets with one of his accounts.

The Marketing Department

Every radio station wants to have as many listeners as possible. If no one listened to the station, who would want to buy advertising time? How would the station stay in business? So just as the sales department's accounts advertise their products on the radio, the radio station advertises itself —over the radio, on billboards, on television, and in newspapers and magazines.

A large radio station like this one usually hires an **advertising agency** to assist with its ad program. What should be advertised, where, and when is decided by the station's marketing department and the ad agency working together.

When the ad agency comes up with an advertising idea, it submits sketches like this one to the station's marketing department for approval.

The marketing department also prepares materials, like brochures or biographies of popular announcers, that will help the sales department sell radio time to its accounts. And finally, the marketing department conducts research such as analyzing program popularity ratings or surveying the station's audience to learn what people want to hear.

The marketing director watches a film for a television commercial with a person from the ad agency. At this stage they can still make changes in the commercial if they are not happy with it.

There are about 9,000 radio stations operating in the United States and over 25,000 radio stations around the world. People living in metropolitan areas can select radio programs from dozens of stations. What they select depends on more than a good marketing department. To make a radio station successful, the station needs popular announcers, good producers, and knowledgeable technicians. It needs an extensive music library, an efficient newsroom and weather center, and a productive sales department. It needs all of these people working together morning, noon, and often, night.

Glossary

accounts: clients, such as supermarkets and other businesses, that purchase radio time for advertising their goods or services

advertising agency: a company whose business is to assist other companies in creating their advertising campaigns

announcers: the people we regularly hear talking on the radio as they introduce music, deliver commercials, or conduct interviews

announcer's copybook: a book filled with scripts for the announcements and commercials that an announcer reads on the air

control room: the room in which a technician works during a radio broadcast

current surface maps: diagrams of weather conditions that come into the weather center over a current surface maps machine

disc jockey: another word for announcer. Most disc jockeys have programs that are mainly music.

DOS: the Daily Operating Schedule, a list of everything that is to happen while a radio station is on the air

edit: to choose which sections of a story or a tape should be broadcast and which should not

engineer: see technician

general manager: the person in charge of a radio station

meteorologist: weather forecaster

national weather wire: a service that sends weather reports and forecasts to radio stations over teletypewriters

newscaster: a person who delivers regular news programs on the air

news director: the person in charge of the news department and all the people who work in it, including reporters, newscasters, and news editors

news editor: a person who oversees the work of reporters and, along with the news director, decides which news stories will be reported on the air

precipitation: wet weather such as snow or rain

prerecord: to record in advance

producers: people who help create and organize radio programs

program director: the person in charge of programming

remote broadcasts: live broadcasts that take place outside the radio station

reporters: people who gather news information

splice: to add parts to or remove parts from a tape by cutting the tape with a razor, then taping the tape back together

sportscaster: an announcer who delivers sports programs

spotter: a person who helps the sportscaster by identifying players during a game

statistician: a person who provides the sportscaster with information about the players in a game

technician: a person who plays the records and runs the equipment at a large station

teletypewriter: a machine that receives news and other information in a radio station. This information is typewritten and can be ripped off the machine for up-to-the-minute reporting.

traffic manager: the person who keeps track of programs, interviews, and everything else that goes on the air and prepares the DOS

weather radar screens: television screens that show the movement of precipitation over an area